Setting theWastebasket On FIRE

When Chickens Bloom in the Widow's Garden

By BONNIE SIMON

SETTING THE WASTEBASKET ON FIRE: WHEN CHICKENS
BLOOM IN THE WIDOW'S GARDEN

Published by
Hungry Chicken Homestead
Colorado Springs, Colorado
727-580-3415

Editor: Colleen Kern
Cover Design & Formatting: Lisa Guyaz
ISBN: 979-8-218-26536-6
First edition. January 30, 2024. First Printing. January 30, 2024

Author Note

How long does it take to write a book? A long time, especially if you're writing 500 words at a time.

The process of writing this book began in 2008 when my now-late-husband, Dave, got sick. A friend of ours set up a blog so I wouldn't have to spend all my time on the phone updating people about Dave's condition. We would write about whatever was happening, and people would read it as they found time. In those days, this was a brilliant innovation. One that I was grateful for under the circumstances.

My first entries were more like captain's logs than essays. However, as the situation became more dire, I began writing with fewer numbers and more feeling. Writing about what had happened and how I felt, made me feel better. I felt supported by the beautiful, caring comments people left. We were able to commiserate through the connection of that simple blog in a way I didn't expect.

The blog tapered off after Dave's death; however, I continued to write. I wrote articles for Toby Bloomberg's AllTheSingleGirlfriends.com and for my own entrepreneurial endeavor called HungryChickenHomestead.com.

Widowhood for me is a journey, moving through ideas and beliefs and consistently trying to answer that persistent question, "Why am I still here?" I didn't know where the path led, but ten years later, I looked back at the blogs I wrote and can now map out where I had been.

Hence, we arrived at this book. Here you have the map of my journey into the unknown. It was not written in chronological order, and the blogs are simply pins on the map of my circuitous journey in a time of confusion.

Like the ancient Israelites, I wandered back and forth in the desert, finding the answer to my question and taking a long, long time to write a book.

I'd like to thank…

Colleen Kern for her editing work. She was the right woman for the job.
Lisa Guyaz for her beautiful cover art.
Clay Worthington for being in the right place at the right time to get me to finish the book.
Toby Bloomberg for her encouragement and publishing of my essays.
The many readers who read drafts and gave me feedback, including my cherished neighbor ladies.
Gail Simon, my mother, for leaving her whole life to stay with me during those awful first few months without Dave. I'll never forget her sacrifice and steadfastness.

And most of all, Steve Simon, my dad, for setting the example of how to write a book, for encouraging me to publish it, and for being proud of me when I finally did it.

Preface - Ticketed Passengers Only

Blog: "Widow" September 19, 2008

"Look, Bonnie," Dave said, last summer, pointing at a budding day lily. "A tomorrow lily."

David E. F--, 45, of Cleveland Heights, passed on yesterday afternoon, surrounded by family and friends. He would probably say he went over the Rainbow Bridge, ratcheting down the tension and drama with typical skill. His beloved Kitty was present when he crossed, and his adoring wife went as far as she could with him.

"Can I walk her down the jetway?" Dave asked the gate attendant at the airport when I was too afraid to get on the plane alone a few years ago. "I'm sorry, sir," replied the attendant. "Ticketed passengers only."

In addition to the widow, Dave is survived by both parents, a sister, a brother, both parents-in-law, a brother-in-law, 2 nieces, 3 nephews, 3 cats, and the many friends he loved.

"It'll be alright, sweetie," I told him before the medical staff removed the life-support tubes. "You have your challenge to meet, and I have mine. We can do this."

Dave was the bravest man I ever knew. He knew what he believed yet heard challenges with an open mind. He wasn't afraid to be who he was, even when that meant going against expectations. He valued his relationships and would work mightily to do things that were important to those he loved. He treated everyone with kindness and respect and approached life with an unmatched sense of good humor. I seldom saw him get angry. He knew how to accept life for what it was, and he could accept other people as is, with all their flaws.

That's a good thing because I have plenty of flaws. In the 12 years we were married, Dave taught me how to be calm. He was my anchor, showing me how to let things be as they were without feeling that a catastrophe was on the horizon. And even after he got sick, which qualifies as a real catastrophe, he didn't lose his equanimity, kindness, or humor. If we handled this situation with dignity and grace, it was only because I followed Dave's lead. He had an uncommon ability to accept whatever came his way without anger or blame.

"It's alright," I said and kissed his forehead. He stopped the futile gasping for breath. And his family and I watched his heart rate drop on the monitor. The morphine protected him from pain, but my heart pounded enough for us both.

Dave met his challenge yesterday, and today, I must meet mine, even if all it can mean right now is continuing to breathe. I only hope I can match the courageous humility with which Dave met his.

The funeral will probably be on Sunday. I will post the time and place here later today. Please come if you can. I want Dave to be able to look down at us and see how many people cared that he was here. These things mattered to Dave. Five years ago, I held a 40th birthday party for him. He was surprised and delighted that just about everyone invited showed up. If he sees us now, I know he would be just as delighted to see people attend another event in his honor.

"Death doesn't end relationships," said the rabbi at Dave's bedside. "It changes them, but it doesn't end them." I'll carry Dave with me from here on out. My life is better for having known him, and I wouldn't have traded those 12 years for anything.

The Tomorrow Lilies

I know what you're wondering:

"Is it okay to ask what happened?"

I hear this question a lot.

It's perfectly alright.

However, please understand that Dave's illness and death are the end of one story. And while I don't want to relive the ending, it is interwoven in this tale. Its ending generated a new beginning, a new story.

I don't want to go back there again. Once was enough. However, I'll share with you this small piece of the story.

Yes, It's Alright to Ask

It was 2008. My career was on the upswing, and I was enjoying my rising star at the Fortune 50 company, where Dave and I worked in the same IT department. After many years of putting in the work and continually learning, I had found my place, my niche in the corporate world—finally building the career I thought I wanted since graduate school.

Dave and I had a good life. We had an intriguing old house, and we were fixing it up. I had taken up gardening, and we were experimenting with ways to save energy. Together, we walked, and fixed things, and enjoyed our pursuit of simplicity.

In the summer, Dave began feeling unwell regularly. So, he visited a couple of doctors. We thought he had diverticulitis, a common condition among men in midlife. We weren't worried. Something like that doesn't interfere with the dreams of growing old together.

We went about our business, unaware that the real problem would change everything.

When the first round of antibiotics didn't really help, our family doctor ordered further testing. And so it was, that one day, I came home from a team picnic to learn Dave's doctor had found out his white blood cell count was high. Very, very high.

As we tried to process the news, Dave hugged me in the driveway.

"I'm scared," he admitted.

The following week, we went to a hematologist and came home with a diagnosis of acute lymphocytic leukemia.

A Short History of Hospitalization

Like I mentioned before, I don't really want to go back there. It will be enough to say that Dave went into the hospital, chose a six-week regimen of chemotherapy, and got pneumonia at the end of it.

After two weeks in the ICU, our formerly optimistic doctors convened a meeting with me and Dave's family, where we had to decide how to proceed.

I came out of that meeting and went straight to Dave's room.

"We have a new challenge," I told him as I explained the situation.

"Your challenge is to figure out how to die, and mine is to figure out how to live without you."

He had "very bad leukemia," as one of his doctors commented at the end. Despite the heroic actions of doctors, nurses, and even the stunningly generous strangers who donated their own white blood cells, he couldn't overcome the assault on his lungs.

Dave died on September 18, 2008, at the age of 45, launching me into what I think of as Part II of my life.

Why Am I Still Here?

It's been more than a decade since that day. And one thing strikes me as particularly consistent—the question that never goes away.

It started the day after Dave's death. I woke up surprised and would wake up surprised nearly every morning for years. The same exact phrase would echo through my mind.

"Why am I still here?"

For more than 12 years, Dave and I had been a team. We had made decisions together, taken risks together, made sacrifices together…

How could I possibly still be here when the other half of my team was gone?

Why was I still here?

Though it didn't stop the question, the answer came in the form of a memory I referenced in my "Widow" essay on our blog.

It's the late 1990s, and I have to go to Atlanta to visit my terminally ill grandmother. I'm terrified to fly and sobbing as Dave walks me to the jetway.

"Can I walk her to the plane?" he asks the agent.
"I'm sorry, sir," he replies.
"Ticketed passengers only."

I didn't have a ticket to wherever it was that Dave
went. I couldn't go with him, and there was nothing I
could do to change it.

Making Meaning from Catastrophe

What can you do when life puts up a brick wall?

I couldn't change what happened. All I could do was
change the meaning of the question.

Why am I still here?

Blog: "Living a Dangerous Life" April 20, 2011

Everyone knows it's dangerous to, let's say, ride a motorcycle
or eat saturated fat, but somehow, we miss the inherent
danger of being alive.

My husband died of acute leukemia. In June of 2008, we were
living ordinary lives. In July, I took Dave to the doctor for
what we thought was diverticulitis, common to 45-year-old
men and easy to cure. In August, he was trapped in the
hospital on chemotherapy. And by the end of September, he
was gone. The whole hospital episode, from diagnosis to
death, took six weeks.

Is it any wonder that it seems to me that we barely control
anything in our lives? Trouble will find you even if you're

perfectly still. What kind of world is this? The raw truth is that it's a world where the person you need the most can be taken from you with no warning.

It's awfully harsh, I know, and no one wants to hear this. "They did something wrong." We all want to think to ourselves. But don't blame me, I'm just the bearer of bad news. Nobody knows why people get leukemia. A person doesn't get hit by a car because of careful deliberation. Lightning never explains itself. Some things happen for no reason. Or at least a reason we mere mortals could never hope to understand.

It's alright, though. Good things happen for no reason too. Don't forget that.

After Dave died, nothing made sense. I had seen or talked to him nearly every day for 13 years, and I knew he would never leave me if he could help it. And then he vanished before my very eyes. My heart was certain I would be allowed to follow.

It was like being in a waiting room. I was waiting to disappear, to vanish, to be stirred into the medium of the universe, like sugar into iced tea. "Why am I still here?" I would ask myself, surprised, a dozen times a day.

I refer to those days as the "insane period" of widowhood. I jumped right back into the dating pool, contrary to all decency, where no doubt I was subconsciously trying to duck the horror of what had happened. I got a new job. I remodeled and then sold the house. I traveled. I saw friends. I went to the gym every day and never went home until after dark.

As long as I was moving, I wasn't in that hospital room anymore, watching Dave suffer.

My friends circled around, protecting me, helping me, and making sure I didn't self-destruct. People I barely knew brought me food and showed up when I needed them. Friends in different states opened their homes, giving me a place to get away. Even the company I worked for stepped up to the plate in its impersonal and benevolent way, making it possible for me to move away from the ghosts of my old life.

The Insane Phase

My experience of widowhood is that it did, in fact, start with a phase of insanity. I hear that this is pretty common. Immediately after an abrupt loss, people often seem to the outside world to have lost their senses. Some people fall for scams—others make what appear to be uncharacteristic decisions.

I'm no psychologist, and I can't explain how the brain handles loss. I've read that the conscious mind disconnects from its emotions, to some extent, to protect itself.

I can believe that. It would be impossible to function and adapt otherwise.

My experience was one of shifting boundaries. When you think about your life and what you believe about the world, certain things just seem, with absolute certainty, that they must be true. Other things seem like they simply can't be true. You expect people to behave

a certain way and your immediate world to be
relatively stable.

Though sometimes we indeed question the reality of
that stability, we try hard to believe in it. Otherwise, we
get too anxious! I've always been prone to anxiety, and
sometimes, over the course of our marriage, I would
awaken in the middle of the night, startled, and I'd
wake Dave up in terror.

"I'm afraid you'll die." I would whisper plaintively
after explaining my nightmare.

He would smile reassuringly, "I won't die."

Doesn't that say it all?

He was certain he wouldn't die, at least not for another
30 years or so. And in the daylight, I was certain too.
How many people in your acquaintance have died
before age 50? Not many, if you're lucky. How could
we live if we couldn't take for granted that we, and the
people we love, would wake up tomorrow?

When he did die, it was contrary to everything I knew
about the world. If my 45-year-old husband could die,
then it seemed as though anything else could happen
too. All of the boundaries on what was possible or
impossible dissolved.

All bets were off. Anything could happen.

As long as I kept moving, I could manage. I went back to work almost immediately, setting myself up for some awkward situations. However, I couldn't see how staying home in bed was going to make things better.

One morning, as I stood in line for coffee in the cafeteria, a colleague, who hadn't been keeping up with the blog, asked me how Dave was doing.

"Oh," I responded as if she had asked me how a project was going. "He died."

I was unaccustomed to handling other people's feelings about us, but now I had become Dave's representative in the world. It was my job to tell them what had happened.

Another friend called with the same question. "I just wanted to call and ask how Dave is doing," she said. People were so kind about checking in on us.

I did better this time. "I'm so sorry, I have bad news," I began and paused. She burst into tears, knowing what I was going to say next.

I didn't cry, myself. I cried only once. I fell down a short flight of stairs one morning after my family had left. I wasn't hurt, but I don't think I've ever felt so alone as in that moment. That's when the tears came.

Caretaker

Our house had been too big for the two of us and our three cats. We had lived in a big, three-story house in an urban suburb. We used to laugh about how we had 3,000 square feet, and yet, most of the time, we would all be together in the same room.

I couldn't sleep in the bedroom anymore after the death. So, I retired to the third floor. I had never felt safe living alone. So, at night, Spot the Cat, and I would search the house for intruders. I told Spot we were hunting for monsters, and if we found one, we would make monster soup. Spot seemed satisfied with this bravado and would poke his nose into corners as we went from room to room. We never found anything, but it made me feel more secure.

Once the monster search was done, all three cats would escort me as I climbed the attic stairs and got ready for bed. What began as a way to avoid sleeping in the bedroom where Dave's absence was most palpable, over time, turned me into a detached caretaker of what had once been our home.

I wanted to sell the house and move to Colorado. A far-away place I had never seen, and where the ghosts of our old life couldn't follow. I accepted a job, and all that was left was to sell the house. It was early 2009, during the trough of the housing depression. My very competent Realtor explained that the home would have to be staged. Everything had to be painted, and the carpets would have to be removed.

Contractors came and went for weeks, slowly transforming the house from "Bonnie and Dave's home" to "a must-see spotless 1920s-era colonial." I clung to the idea of the future. All day and night, I would daydream of mountains and the desert. I immersed myself in maps and apartment websites. Twice, the company sent me to Colorado to look for a place to live. In the 300 square feet of the hotel room, I felt the relief and safety similar to waking up from a nightmare.

Yet, I would return home each time to the same nightmare. Spot and Kitty and Snowball, and I lived in the attic, the caretakers of what would soon be someone else's home, but could never be a home to us again.

Leaving

I started the van after the moving truck left and suddenly remembered.

I left a litter box in an upstairs bedroom!

I didn't want to go in again. But I turned off the van, grimly climbed the stairs for the last time, and brought the box down for the trash without looking right or left.

Usually, people look around one last time before moving away and feel sad, even if they are excited to move on.

Not me. I blamed the house somehow—the way a cat blames a litter box for any pain experienced there.

Nothing would do but to get away from it as fast as I could.

I restarted the van, drove away, and never looked back.

Chapter 1: Cats in a House of Mourning

Blog: "House of Mourning" July 5, 2011

This is a house of mourning, even if you can't see it among the brightly colored ceramic lizards or hear it in the laughter.

I have woven mourning into every house I've lived in since the death of my husband in 2008. It flickers like dappled sunlight, casting shadows with the death of each cat who was part of our home, with every new chicken in the yard or farm skill learned, with the introduction of every potential long-term boyfriend.

Our old life slips away like hands reluctantly unclasping. Like the sun at the summer solstice, an era sets slowly.

Sometimes, I sit outside at the most recent grave and talk to Spot. I tell him things I never told him when he skulked around the house, catching mice and stealing Snowball's food. I tell him how I scolded the vet for the failure to help me provide palliative care in the way I should have scolded Dave's doctors for the invasive treatments past the point of diminishing returns. I apologize for not being able to arrange an easier death for him. I talk about how sometimes I feel as if I could lie down in the dirt next to his grave and simply turn to dust.

It hasn't happened yet. Even though when I'm still, I feel as if I could simply fade into the universe, I still don't turn to dust. A friend gives me a hard time about doing what I "have" to do instead of what I "want" to do, but these days the two words merge together. My house, my business, and my animals provide the skin that keeps me together. I bustle around, constantly moving, building, feeding, and caring. The day begins and ends with the sun, and I fall asleep at night, exhausted and solid.

Time is like a strong wind, and sometimes we need to march right into it, eyes straight ahead and jaw set, just to prove we have weight and heft in the world. We need to show what is inside on our outsides, like a tattoo. Inside, I have become the solitary and determined pioneer woman with her shotgun, guarding her homestead. Outside, I learn to keep rain, predators, and creditors at bay by myself. Inside, I grit my teeth, stand my ground, and hold the line against an unpredictable world. Outside, I compete with the strongest women at the gym, conquer my distaste for marketing, and learn to tactfully say no to attractive men who aren't good for me.

We can't stop time by denying its passing. We can't stop loss by denying we ever cared. We can accept the changes, or we can turn to dust.

The sun shines through the elm leaves onto Spot's grave in my backyard, just as it shines through the maple leaves on Dave's grave some 1,500 miles away. The young chickens and elderly cats playfully stalk each other. The pea plants soften into white-flowered tendrils, shading the nascent lettuce. I test a riot of recipes in the kitchen, and friends come and go, sampling the food, drinking all the wine, and laughing. The ceramic lizards hold still, the only ones truly frozen in time.

Cats

At the end of the day, when you close the door on the world, who is there?

Maybe you have a house full of people, a spouse, children, friends.

I had the cats. At the end of the day, it was me and them. Every day, I thanked God for them because, without those cats, my whole family was gone.

Kitty, Snowball, and Spot slowed the loss and made it more bearable. Our world had been made up of five of us, two humans, and three lively little comedians. After Dave was gone, it was made up of one human and three confused little comforters.

I moved to Colorado and bought a house for us. I stocked the yard with chickens to keep us entertained. Every morning, I would wake up relieved that the four of us were safe in our Colorado home, far from the horror of what had happened.

But cats don't live forever. And these cats, the ones I called the "Traveling Cats" because they had made the cross-country trip with me, were already past ten years old.

One by one, they crossed the Rainbow Bridge.
One by one, they left me and went to Dave.

I can see them now. Dave resting on a cloud in Heaven with the Traveling Cats nestled around him, just like they were in life. When it's my turn to go, and I see them again, I'll run as fast as I can to join the snuggling, and tell them all about my long, long day without them.

It's 93 degrees, and the sun is relentless. It's hard to dig in the dry Colorado dirt, but I've done this before. I know I'll need the rubber mallet and a tent stake to pry out the rocks. I'll need the square shovel to shave down the sides, making room for the box, and the big shovel to carry out the loosened dirt.

The sharp shovel cuts through the tree roots, and I feel every blow and break. The roots, sheathed in red, scream a painful mess of color into the soil. I don't know which tree I've severed, lilac, elm, or fir, but I know how it feels.

We called Snowball "the Last Cat Standing." He lived the longest of the three and a full year past the time of the first cat's death. Spot, the first, died traumatically under the bed. He died that way because I didn't know what to do. I didn't know how to arrange a peaceful death for him, and I didn't know how to cross that bridge into the inevitable march into the loss of my three beloved feline companions.

After Dave died, the cats were what remained of my family. The loss of a husband means the loss of an intimate world, the world that remains in the house when night falls, and the doors are all closed. It means the loss of a haven because the house fills with ghosts. Every object is a memory, and the gap between what was and what is hovers over the home like a storm cloud.

The cats filled the gap. Dave was gone, but they remained through all the transition and trauma.

Without them, I am on my own. My link to the safety and pleasure of that time in my life is gone. New cats prance around the house and sleep in the bed. They are adorable and comforting but rootless strangers with no tie to the past.

I knew this leg of the journey was coming. For months I had eyed the tiny graveyard with dread, knowing someday soon, a third and final grave would be needed. And then, expected, but almost without warning, that time came.

Somehow, it's especially hard to lose Snowball. I rescued him 16 years ago in a parking lot where he was trying to eat a potato pancake. He's never tried to eat one since, and I know he was hungry. I had waited a long time with him that day, uncertain, reluctant to leave him. A shy cat, he eventually chose to trust me enough to jump into my car and let me take him home.

I've taken that trust seriously and took him to the vet because he seemed to be having trouble breathing. I had promised him

I wouldn't let him suffocate like Spot did. Unlike Spot, I wouldn't let him down.

I can't shake the memory of him trustingly walking towards me that morning, slowly on his arthritic legs, as I sat on the bench in the graveyard where I'd buried the others.

Despite wanting desperately to spare myself the journey, somehow, I didn't let him down. We had a nice morning, waiting for the vet's office to open. We sat together outside in the coolness of the morning air. I petted him. I talked to him. He looked at me, straight in the eyes, as if he knew too, and at 8:15 am, he let me put him in the carrier.

When Dave was dying, part of the ritual asked me to forgive him for everything I might need to forgive him for. Now I need the dead to come back for a minute and say, "Hey. It's okay. You did the best you could for us. You even buried us with your own hands. We're alright. It's okay to let us be where we are. It's alright for you to focus on the living."

But I'm afraid of ghosts, and they don't come. I dig the graves, hold the funerals, write the memorial essays, and do whatever I can to honor them. Once someone is gone, all you can do is honor the memory, straddling the gap between the living and the dead. Every homecoming feels like a head-on collision when I remember again that Snowball isn't here.

A homestead cat deserves a homestead burial, with a grave full of my tears and sweat and a favorite toy showing how much we loved him. I wish I could have dug Dave's grave too. As always, I dig all afternoon, burying the body by

Why Am I Still Here?

I remember Dave lying in that stupid hospital bed,
telling me he regretted that we never took a Mississippi
River cruise. Believe me, if I could go back in time, then
I would insist that we take that trip.

You can't go back, however. The past is fixed into place
and immovable. Only the future is still malleable. For
some reason, I'm still here, and though I can barely fill
in the details of that awful time of my life, though I can
still barely move in my memories, time moves forward,
and I move with it.

Friends, family, cats, and chickens fill my life. Like
anyone else, I live, and I work, and I play. The question
has changed in the way words and phrases change
meaning over time as you experience new things. What
used to mean, "How could I still be here when Dave is
gone?" had to evolve as it became more and more
obvious that I am still alive.

For reasons unknown to me, I have been granted the
time that Dave didn't get. It's incontrovertible that
some things can only be accomplished by the living.
The dead are too far from us to offer small kindnesses,
encourage others, or nudge the world in other ways

toward being a better place. Every single one of us on this side of the grave can do something of meaning and goodness.

But the knowledge of how fleeting all this is has been indelibly impressed on me.

After I survived to see my own 45th birthday and began to live the years past the age Dave had been when he died. An incomprehensible idea to me before that birthday, the question took on a new shape. It began to mean: What should I do with this time? What meaning does this time have? What meaning can I give it?

Don't waste your life.

By all means, take for granted that you'll wake up in the morning and rest secure in the illusion that you're not really mortal like the rest of us.

But for the love of God, don't waste your life.

Blog: "Notes from the Little Graveyard" March 15, 2013

Are there greater pleasures than a morning in springtime?

I slept late. I admit it. Nothing can induce me to get out of bed early on a cloudy morning; not Patience's vigorous attempts to conquer my feet, not Mr. Pickles' loud purring, nor the knowledge that Roxanne Chicken is making her morning foray into more and more remote places in the garage and knowing I'll have to figure out how to retrieve her.

When I finally got out of bed and retrieved the Garage Chicken, I realized we don't have this trait of morning laziness in common.

Chickens don't like to miss anything. Every morning, I bring Roxanne outside and give her some almond bits while I make sure we have enough feed and water for everyone. The rest of the flock mobs the chicken door in the coop. I've written before how they seem to feel they've been unjustly imprisoned, and they never change their minds.

In fact, this very morning, I witnessed Specklehead come running out of the coop a few minutes after the jailbreak with great concern and eagerness to join the flock. She had been held up by Nature's call to lay an egg.

The cats come outside with me, too. I'm not in favor of letting my cats roam the neighborhood—they have no money or ID, and I can't bear not knowing where they are. My last batch of beloved cats, Kitty, Snowball, and Spot, were very much in favor of roaming in their younger days, which led to something of a political dispute between us. However, Patience and Mr. Pickles prefer to spend their time with me in the backyard. If I go in, Pickles comes with me, and Patience appears on the deck minutes later, distressed at being left alone.

At this very moment, the air is still, and cool. Underneath the roar of an airplane and the highway noise, the chirping of small birds outlines the morning silence.

Together, we revel in the loveliness of the morning. The chickens have resumed their daily scratch-and-peck routine— the cats are exploring the straw-covered ground (stopping only to chew on the ends of rosebushes). And me?

I am breathing in the stillness of the Homestead on an early spring morning, savoring a sweetness heightened by what I know to be true—what my big monkey brain alone, among all the brains in the yard, tells me.

It won't last. As the tiny graveyard near the fence mutely notes, none of it will last.

Treasure it while you can.

Chapter 2: The Challenge

Don't you love farmers' markets? I used to go to one in Cleveland every week. I would walk or bike the couple of miles to the market and spend the morning buying, eating, and socializing with farmers.

After Dave's death, I found myself explaining to them why I hadn't been there for a few weeks. A conversation I had with Karen was typical.

"We haven't seen you in a while," she stated. "We missed you."

"Oh," I responded awkwardly, closely inspecting a cabbage, though my skill at informing people about what had happened was improving. "Yes… you see, my husband got very sick, and I was taking care of him."

"Oh my," she said sympathetically. "How is he?"

I frowned, looking grim. "He didn't make it. He passed away on September 18."

Farmers are some of the most remarkable people I've met anywhere. She didn't change the subject awkwardly or even look surprised. Without missing a beat, she nodded knowingly, and said simply, "I'm so sorry."

She asked a few questions about what had happened, and then, when I started to falter, changed the subject back to cabbage.

The next week, Karen gave me a condolence card. I was touched that she remembered and flabbergasted at how smoothly she handled this ponderous subject.

How did she do that? I experienced that kind of thing again and again with farmers. They didn't fear discussions of death the way other people seemed to. They weren't uncomfortable—they related easily, and they could respond without making me feel like some sort of outlier in the human experience.

Maybe, just maybe, they even knew why I was still here!

I wanted to know what they knew. Once I was settled into my own home in Colorado and it was safe to experiment, I set out to solve that mystery.

Blog: "Losing Chickens" October 19, 2014

We are down to five hens. We started the summer with nine, but now we only have five. While I'm finding this quite distressing, it's interesting to note that the chickens are behaving with exactly the same exuberance they have every day.

You're probably wondering what happened. Did they get attacked by those pesky raccoons who have been breaking into feed buckets? Did someone finally steal them?

No. They just died. One by one, even with the help of the veterinarian, they died on their own.

Marshmallow laid an egg one day and expired. I found her and the egg in the nest box. Redhead's comb turned purple, and then I found her one morning by the garden fence. Pumpkin got some sort of mass in her belly that compressed her digestion. And yesterday, Specklehead... well, Specklehead hadn't been eating. Her comb was pale, and she was lethargic. I gave her some egg to eat, hoping to get some protein into her, and, just like that, she died.

It was quite upsetting. I'm still pretty shaken up.

I think I understand now why some people don't want to feel anything about chickens. They want them to be "just chickens," entities without feelings or personalities. As anyone who has ever met a live chicken knows, these things are not true, but if they were, then we wouldn't have to mourn the loss of each hilarious, exuberant bird.

It's too late for me, though. I already know the truth, and it disturbs me that these little bird friends whom I talked to and played with and cared for are gone. In general, these silly animals who try to eat my hat and steal grapes out of my hands, live for a powerful flash and then fade out of existence like lightning on a seemingly clear night. I know they don't live long, and I don't want to fear their demise. I want to understand that the difference between life and death is ultimately out of my hands; that my responsibility is to treat them well and let them be birds. But if a person is to permit her own feelings, then every death is going to sting, whether she accepts it as part of life or not.

I miss them and marvel at how the other birds just go on being birds. They might rearrange where they sleep, but they aren't any more or less nice to each other today than they were yesterday. They still stand around preening and come running when I open the door, even though just yesterday, they watched Specklehead's death throes with me. I see no evidence that they now fear the future or feel that anything is different today at all.

They don't, but I do. Sometimes a big brain is no blessing.

Chapter 3: The Chickens of Iniquity

I had an imaginary bargain with Life. I ended that bargain with my move to Colorado.

To this day, I'm not sure why they offered me the job. I will always be grateful to the Lead Engineer who wanted to hire me for a job in Colorado, primarily because it caused the company to pay for a move away from the ghosts in Cleveland.

Ghosts were everywhere after Dave's death, and I just wanted to get away. I couldn't walk down a street without seeing ghosts of the past. "Look! That's where we stopped to admire this weird house!" "Look! Here are the first flowers of spring we waited for every year!"

I love Colorado. It's so much easier to have a life here, away from the ghosts and constant reminders of what was lost.

Once I got to Colorado, I completely revised my personal life. It's often a great surprise to people that just as there is a long list of negative aspects of widowhood, there are also some positive aspects. For example, I can choose where to live without consulting anyone but my loan officer.

Moving across the country in the first year of widowhood and then buying a house clashed dramatically with the standard advice to widows, but I didn't care.

"Don't make any major decisions in the first year," they would say.

"I don't think you understand what's happened here," I would respond. "And maybe you can't, but I'll try to explain."

Up until my widowhood, I had followed all the standard advice: get an education and get a good job with the tacit understanding that my good decisions would lead to a manageable life. Life's job was to, among other things, let me and Dave grow old together.

Have you lived that way too? Do you still?

Naturally, I was angry about the breach in our tacit agreement. Since Life had done such a poor job of keeping up its end of the imaginary bargain, I wasn't going to keep my end up either.

I'm not suggesting that we should throw caution to the wind and dismiss the need to make good decisions for our lives, but sometimes we take this imaginary contract so seriously that we put our dreams on the shelf and avoid reasonable risks so that we're not in breach of contract.

How often have you thought of something you'd love to do, like start a business, or travel, or move somewhere exciting, but you've put it off because of this implied agreement?

I did it a million times, letting internal and external voices tell me I was obliged to live quietly.

It's a lie, of course. There is no bargain.

Life acts in complete freedom, and so can you.

Listening for the Red Army

I was raised to be a hardworking, non-risk-taking, middle-class person, and to this day, I lie awake nights, worried about money for no reason at all.

Does that seem weird to you? Maybe not, maybe we are similar.

Think about it. Do you lie awake worrying about money when disaster is not imminent? Is money the root of whatever is keeping you awake? Or is it a substitute for something more abstract? Money is a big topic of worry and debate for many people, sometimes as the center of a problem and sometimes as a symptom.

As for me, I came from people who escaped the pogroms (mass murders of Jews in Russia and Eastern Europe around the turn of the 20th century). Among those immigrant relatives were people who had major disabilities at a time when disabled people were considered unemployable. In the mid-twentieth century, my progenitors experienced family trauma in times when people didn't talk about such things.

Like many families, my family was overladen with reasons to minimize risk. Instability moved in with us and sat down at the dinner table. We didn't need to go seeking it.

The result? We're a little inflexible. We like to stick with what is known to work.

We are the kind of people who work hard and do everything we can to find security, all while listening for the approach of the Red Army. Trauma like that sticks with families for generations, and money provides a lot of security. Money can move you across the world when people are trying to kill you; it can support you when people dismiss your abilities, and it can keep food on the table when your relationships are in jeopardy.

This attachment to security became an important issue after Dave's death because of the persistent question that never leaves.

Why am I still here?

At first, I was simply surprised to exist. Later, the question became the guiding principle of every risk I

took. If I didn't take risks, how would I ever find the
answer?

Blog: "Why Animals are Better than Computers" March 11,
2013

*Daylight Savings Time has a way of wreaking havoc on
computer systems. I mention this because I set out to post
about events this morning, but I can't get WordPress to post
the pictures. What is a post about food without pictures?*

I blame this on the time change.

*Things like this used to happen twice a year at the big
corporation where I worked for ten years. The computers
didn't know what time it was anymore, and they got all tied
up in knots. Paralyzed with anxiety, they would simply stop,
or they would frantically start doing things that didn't make
any sense.*

Computers are surprisingly rigid about these sorts of things.

*This does not happen on the Homestead. We are very
adaptable. The chickens were pleasantly surprised when I let
them out earlier. The cats and dogs merely wondered if I was
going out of town, which is what usually happens when I get
up early.*

*Even the coffeemaker adapted well, since we just push the
"on" button when we get up.*

Why do we change the time twice a year? It seems like an awful lot of trouble. What time will we eat? How do we know when to get up? How will we remember what time it is in Arizona?

I would write to Congress to suggest they pick a time and stick to it, but they never listen to me. Instead, I'll just post this pictureless essay and spend the day being grateful my homestead is not governed by confused machines. Everything will go pretty smoothly.

Even if no one around here knows what time it is.

My Very Own House

I settled into Mr. M's office. After the initial pleasantries, I explained that I'd like to buy a house.

"Alright," he said, "tell me more. What kind of house are you looking for?"

I had thought about this carefully. "I'd like something in the city, close to downtown," I explained.

Mr. M nodded and scrawled a note on a legal pad. "OK. We can find that. How many bedrooms and bathrooms?" he said without looking up.

"Well," I said, "I'd like something with at least two bedrooms and two bathrooms and no Homeowners' Association."

"No Homeowners' Association?"

"I am buying a house so that I can get chickens, and HOAs hate chickens."

Mr. M stared motionless at the paper for a moment, and then looked up, filling the room with hearty laughter.

"That's the first time I've gotten this kind of request." He smiled, relaxing and shifting in his chair. "Let's see what we can do."

Hatching Hungry Chicken Homestead

In 2010, I found myself driving an hour out of town to a mysterious ranch in search of chicks.

These days, if you want a flock of chickens, you simply go to the hardware store at the right time of year and pick up some week-old chicks. That wasn't the case in 2010 and I had to start with a search on Craigslist.

I found a reputable looking ad and drove to the mysterious ranch.

"Should I do this?" I asked myself, suspiciously eyeing the isolated rural driveway I'd been directed to.

"What if I'm walking into a serial killer's lair? I can see the headline now…. 'Woman Lured to Her Death by Chickens.'"

A dog ran out to the car, wagging his tail in delight, and the man I'd been corresponding with stepped out and waved.

"Alright," I said with resolve. "At least my friends know where I am."

I got out of the car with a cardboard box and greeted this stranger, who turned out to be perfectly normal. We walked to the barn as he explained that he'd ordered a batch of Rhode Island Red chicks through the mail, but the hatchery required a minimum order of 25, and he didn't need that many.

Side note, for those of you who aren't familiar with how we get chickens in the modern world, the United States Postal Service is the usual way. You just have to be available to pick them up as soon as they come in.

"How many do you want?" the stranger asked. We stood over a dry watering trough filled with a tiny city completely inhabited by chicks. The pine-shaving streets, chick feeder buildings, and recreational watering reservoirs made up a setting where dozens of busy little fluffballs were engaged in the daily business of growing themselves into chickens.

"I'll take four," I said, handing him a $20 bill.

"Do you want to pick them out?"

"I...uh... no need," I stammered, trying to pretend this wasn't the first time I'd ever been in the presence of a live chicken. "They all look healthy. You can pick them."

He scooped up four chicks, put them in the cardboard box, and off we went. They chirped every time the sun came out during the hour drive.

And I sang to them the whole way home.

Blog: "Mock Pickup Truck" November 14, 2010

Today, I want to write about the car. It is a typical suburban small car, a slightly beat up 2002 Toyota Prius. It even has the required crack in the windshield that seems to be a state law in Colorado, judging by how common it is.

I love living in Colorado because it's a place where no one flinches at the dust on my car or on my fancy shoes. Not that I ever wear fancy shoes. I had a closet full of skirts when I lived back east and shoes to go with them, but they are languishing now. Most are too fancy and draw unwanted attention. "Who is that uncomfortably dressed woman?" the passersby would say to each other. "How will she ride a bike in that outfit?". Even my non-fancy skirts are impractical now since every morning starts out with chicken-related chores.

And chicken chores mean straw!

Since chickens are the ultimate omnivores, I needed an insulating material for their coop that was either edible or unappetizing. I thought maybe Cheetos would be good since they meet both criteria, but they can be expensive. Chickens will eat Styrofoam like it was candy, so that was out. Fiberglass looks too much like cotton candy, and they would probably have eaten that too. I even considered cotton candy, since it would attract ants, a fine and exciting chicken treat, but it would just melt the first time it rained.

Straw turned out to be the best option; an insulating material and playground all rolled into one! As soon as I untied the first bale, they jumped right in and started scratching at it with their feet and pecking around for bugs. This went on for days. It's our first chicken toy!

That brings me back to my typical suburban subcompact car, which is now covered with straw on the inside. I like it. I pretend it's a pickup truck and my street is a dirt road. Actually, sometimes it is a dirt road. The city has come out twice in the last four months and ground up the pavement, thoughtfully tailoring it to my rustic neighborhood fantasies.

I love living in Colorado. This is what I always wanted; a place where my backyard livestock, my mock pickup, and the wild chickens of my imagination fit right in.

Dismantling the Cubicle

I found a house and continued to dutifully go to work in the cubicle every day. And every day, I would stare out the window and wonder what the chickens were doing.

I knew what they were doing! They were growing! Each day, I would come home and find that they were bigger than when I left in the morning.

My last job at the corporation was more than I could stand. The other people on the team and I didn't get along very well. I resented variations in the schedule and felt like going to work was a big waste of time. It seemed as if the job left a hole in my day that should have been filled with chickens.

Unfortunately, I was scared to quit, and my terror was stubborn. Anybody else would have known it was time to quit the day I called my boss with the following reason for my absence.

"I'm afraid I can't come in today," I said, in a good imitation of someone with a normal reason for needing to work at home. "We had a big snowstorm last night, and it's extremely cold outside."

My boss didn't seem surprised by this. Northern Colorado Springs can be treacherous in the winter. "So, the roads are icy?" he asked.

"Um… well … no," I said slowly, concerned that I was going to have to drop the facade. "Actually, I can't come in because my chicken coop is too cold, and the chickens are in the garage. I can't leave them."

Dead silence on the phone. And then the uproarious laughter I had hoped for.

A shout of "Save the chickens!" came through the line.

I really should have known then, that my cubicle time was coming to an end.

Blog: "Very Cold Days" January 2, 2011

Very Cold Day #1

Everyone survived the night pretty well, including the baked sweet potato I put in the coop to add warmth. The chickens did not eat it, suggesting it was a welcome companion.

They also seemed to appreciate that I covered their run with plastic sheeting to keep out the wind and snow. That made it easier this morning, when it was zero degrees, to eat their morning oatmeal. I have to crawl into the coop now to open and close the inner door, but honestly, it's more comfortable messing with the latch with some shelter from the wind.

In sum, they survived the night, ate breakfast, and went right back to bed. Today is forecast to be around ten degrees with overnight temps below zero. I wonder if chickens get cabin (coop) fever.

Very Cold Day #2

It was minus something (maybe -9 degrees) last night and didn't quite make it to 20 degrees today. The sweet potato has been mauled. It appears to have been demoted from Companion status to Food status. Chickens can be ruthless.

The birds seem thirsty. I bring out water every few hours, which freezes before the next watering time. They all stand around and drink as if delaying the next leg of a race. Specklehead has transferred her determination to eat hardware to a determination to eat ice. She picks up chips, bashes them on the ground, and eats the shards. I even saw her plunge one unfortunate chip of ice into the water bowl, where she pecked at it until it came apart. Ruthless, I tell you.

No one knows how the chicken brain works. After the sun set, all the other chickens had gone to bed, but she was still pecking away at the half-frozen water bowl. I have no idea why she has decided it's a good idea to eat ice on the coldest day she's ever seen. When she put her foot in the water to improve her aim, I finally picked her up and sent her to bed with an admonishment to avoid encasing her feet in ice. This is the problem with having been hatched in an incubator. Her mother never had a chance to tell her to keep her feet dry.

Everyone seems to be handling the cold temperatures well. Someone even laid an egg! It's supposed to be zero again tonight, but it will warm up to 39° tomorrow. We're all looking forward to that!

I had an idea that my tenure with the corporation was coming to a close, though I couldn't yet bring myself to take the final step of separating from them.

It's not really surprising.

Not only was I contemplating taking the biggest risk of my life, but I was also ending an era. For ten years, Dave and I had worked for that corporation. We'd driven to work together and mulled over the wisdom of frequent reorganizations. Our lives had been tied up tightly with that one big business.

Looking back, I see the time between my move to Colorado and the day I quit as a kind of "resting space," similar to the Israelites in the desert. My mind and my activities wandered this way and that as I tried to make sense of my identity again.

I used the time to prepare for what would happen when I quit my job and crossed the river into a life completely of my own making.

New Skills

I knew absolutely nothing about making a living except for how to get a job. I thought, correctly, that it might be a good idea to take a class. And so, I enrolled in a

semester-long course for entrepreneurs at the local
Small Business Development Center (SBDC).

Learning something new is a great way to motivate
yourself. I embraced this idea from one of my favorite
motivational speakers, Brendon Burchard. I had
embraced this principle for years without articulating
it. However, as I lost interest in my Very Serious Job,
developing and learning about my interests started to
collide with my work.

For example, I developed an obsession with socks in
2005. I would spend hours searching for and studying
the process of knitting socks. Somehow, learning what
a "gusset" was and how to make one made me feel
alive like nothing else.

One day, I was sitting at my desk, deeply engaged with
a website called Socks 101, when I heard the voice of
my manager's manager behind me.

"Bonnie, can you explain these numbers to me?" he
inquired, handing me a report as I whirled around,
surprised.

I blushed as deeply as if I'd been committing a heinous
crime.

"You caught me," I mumbled. "I'm reading about socks
on company time."

He laughed, as only a manager who was relieved not to have to report an employee for creating a hostile work environment can do. "That's OK," he said, with a trace of awkwardness. "Now, about this report...."

I should have knitted him a gift for Christmas.

I'm taking a business class at the local SBDC, and they asked me to present the chapters on management to the class. "How," I thought to myself, "did I get assigned the most boring topic on the list?"

I'm taking this class for a business I haven't actually started yet. I can't see far enough into it to envision any employees I would need to manage. "OK," I tell myself, "what about partnerships or outsourcing relationships?"

And that's when I realized all my employees are chickens.

Well, most of them, anyway. Snowball the Cat guards the kitchen.

My point is, I am managing them by the book. The identified task is egg production, which I have firmly delegated to them. I set the expectations that they will not peck each other and that they will sleep in the coop.

They do their best to live up to my expectations, especially if I motivate them with corn. I also model what I expect of them by personally refraining from pecking anyone and by sleeping in my big fancy coop every night, just as I expect them to sleep in theirs.

It turns out good management skills are important! After all, I can't lay the eggs myself.

Don't tell the chickens I said that. I'll lose all credibility.

Setting the Wastebasket on Fire

My boss was 1,000 miles away and was mostly patient with my situation. But then I got a phone call that was the last straw.

After too many years of on-call and off-hours work, after devoting so many hours to the office that belonged to my friends, family, and pets, I was simmering with resistance to these relationship-depriving responsibilities. I finally boiled over after I had my own bout with pneumonia. I had been working from home because I couldn't find anyone to cover for me when my beleaguered manager called. He told me he wasn't supposed to approve so much work-from-home time.

This felt like the pinnacle of the company's lack of gratitude for all I had sacrificed for it. I was home with pneumonia, working on their business, and they had the gall to tell my boss not to approve my time off? I don't know if that's really quite how it happened behind the scenes, but I quit a few days later.

I quit patiently and professionally, but it was all an act. Right after I quit, while I was still seething with anger and vitriol, I emailed a friend to tell him what happened.

I must not have attempted to hide how upset I was. He responded, "And did you set the wastebasket on fire on your way out?"

I'm sorry to say that I did not, at least not literally. I've remembered his words because it's such a great metaphor. All that fuel of resentment built up and crammed into an overflowing wastebasket in my mind over all those years, and finally, with one match strike of a phone call, the whole thing exploded into flames.

Only One Regret

While I don't really regret staying out of jail by refraining from committing arson, I do have one regret.

I am truly sorry to say that I did not quit out of a greater sense of mission. I'm too stubbornly risk-averse for that, and I was too afraid that I would not be able to survive without the job.

The simple, unavoidable truth was that I quit because I was angry.

When you work in a corporate environment, they pay you well, but they want a lot for their money. I felt like they owned my attitude, the best of my energy, and my time. Important moments in my relationships were interrupted by the pager. Scheduled technical changes would sometimes fall in the middle of holidays when people wanted to connect with their families, and the corporation's business was always expected to take precedence.

Some people feel OK about this, but I couldn't stand it.

If I learned nothing else from my experience of being widowed, I learned that personal and family time must be respected.

Don't get me wrong. I'm not sorry I worked there. After all, that company moved me across the country when I really needed a place to build a new life. I learned countless valuable things about life, work, and myself while I worked there, but the simple truth was that time was up.

That chapter of my life was done, ready or not.

Blog: "Everybody Out! The Chicken B&B is Closed"
August 7, 2014

The Chicken B&B in my garage closed last month. It is mourned by chickens everywhere (in the backyard). The cats are kind of sad, too.

I, on the other hand, am delighted! Chickens have been spending the night in my garage for a long time. You may have heard me tell the story of the day I had to tell my corporate boss that I couldn't come in because chickens had taken refuge from the subzero temperatures in my garage. Since then, the garage has served as a haven for hot chickens, cold chickens, and chickens who wanted nothing to do with the other chickens.

Things started to get out of hand earlier this year when Stray Chicken joined the flock. She wouldn't sleep in the coop. She insisted on sleeping in a tree. We compromised, and she set up a bedroom in a cage in the garage. Sometimes, however, she preferred to sleep in the baskets on the very highest shelf.

Every night, I would pick her up and put her in the garage when the others started roosting in the coop for the night. This is reasonably manageable with one chicken.

Colleen, the Broody Hen, joined us, and then we had two hens staying in the B&B, which was alright because Colleen never did anything other than sit on her eggs and stare. But, of course, one thing led to another, and two chicks joined her. That made a residency rate of four chickens.

Colleen eventually went back to Easter Egg Acres with her little brood, bringing us back to one manageable chicken in the garage, but then something happened...

Little Red Hen came back to live with us!

Little Red is one of those chickens that makes you shake your head and wonder how you became so soft-hearted. She was about 15 weeks old when she arrived, and she decided that...

a. She was still a chick.

b. I was her mama.

This little chicken spent her first few weeks with us, hiding on the patio from the other hens. It's hard to be the new chicken.

She weaseled her way into sleeping in the garage by being distressed when I tried to put her in the coop. It worked. For weeks, I carried TWO chickens into the garage every night and out again in the morning.

In time, as with all animals, she grew up. It was a bittersweet time. She stopped hiding under me and started stealing hardware to bash on the ground. (I don't know why my hens do that when they reach laying age, but they all do it for a while). One night, I picked up each hen and gently put her in the coop. Stray Chicken looked uncertain for a moment and then marched onto the roost. I was very proud of her.

Little Red Hen perched on a nest box. It was a wobbly spot, but it would do. Since then, she bravely settles into the coop each night...as long as I remember to open the egg door, and she doesn't have to use the chicken door like everybody else.

All things in this world come to an end. At least until the next chicken arrives.

A Foggy Future

Who quits a good job in the middle of a recession? It still sounds crazy to me, but that's exactly what I had done.

I loved every minute spent in my peaceful home with my animal friends. I relished the lightness that came with eliminating the burden of that job, but I still questioned my sanity on an hourly basis.

Think for a moment about how you would feel in those shoes. Would you feel terrified? Elated?

I haven't mentioned my financial situation or the talks I had with my financial adviser prior to quitting because, at a fundamental level, *it doesn't even matter*.

It's nearly impossible to anticipate the true outcome when you make a leap of faith. You don't know how long your money will hold out or whether you'll ever earn another dollar. You have no idea whether you'll lose your house or become a millionaire.

You've never done this before, and the future is wide-open, foggy, and mysterious.

When you cut the rope and set yourself adrift from the perceived security of a corporate job for the first time in your life, you have no idea what is going to happen next. You peer into the future, but it's all still in flux.

You have no way of knowing what will happen. Good or bad.

I was terrified but decided to do it anyway. I had learned my lesson about implied contracts with Life. You can try to stay safe all the time by doing what you think you're supposed to do, but it doesn't work. It's a bad bargain.

I'd had inklings of this before, but Dave's death drove home what still feels like a swindle to me. Somehow, I had really believed that we would be "safe" if we just followed the rules. If we kept our jobs, didn't take too many risks, and made sure everyone liked us, then nothing bad could happen to us.

Ha!

I know it's ridiculous, but I'm still angry. You'll hear me say it all the time.

"If Life isn't going to hold up its end of the bargain, then neither am I!"

The time since then has been a journey of finding out who I am, what I want, and how to take intelligent risks to make my post-widowhood life mean something.

That takes faith, and faith is something you can start developing right now.

Shortly after I left my job, Spot the Cat got sick. Spot was one of three cats who lived with me and Dave.

How did we get three cats? Well, I had one staid female cat, Kitty, when we got married. About a year into the marriage, we acquired Snowball when I found him trying to eat a potato pancake in a parking lot. Since cats don't willingly eat potato pancakes, he was obviously lost. I brought him home, and he became part of the household.

Both cats were young, but Kitty wasn't interested in playing with this upstart vagabond cat. So, when I found Spot at the shelter where I volunteered, I brought him home.

"Snowball needs a playmate," I told Dave, and he reluctantly agreed that was probably true.

It didn't work. Spot moved in, and immediately, he and Snowball became mortal enemies. If Spot tried to snuggle with Snowball, Snowball got up and left. If Snowball tried to have peace, Spot picked a fight.

This went on for 14 years.

When Spot got sick, I had to make a decision. He was the first cat to have a terminal illness, and I had just quit my job. How would I balance my budget with his need for medical care?

I don't think my little friends were afraid to die, but they didn't want to suffer. Being unemployed made me face the reality that keeping them alive with medical technology would have been all about me, not them, and that I couldn't really afford it anyway.

Spot had heart problems that made his chest cavity fill with fluid. Getting it out meant a very expensive visit to the specialists. We only went once. He was terrified at that hospital, and so was I. He would quake in terror, and I would wrestle with my resentment at being left to make this decision alone.

It was a hard decision, but I was a recent widow, and good at being grimly decisive. I decided that each cat would get one lifesaving visit to the cat medical specialists. The second time, I would spare them the medical treatments and let them go.

Blog: "Resting Spot" June 8, 2011

Mr. Spot, one of our beloved cats, died on Thursday morning.

He died in the way of his choosing, at home, under the bed, where he felt safe. He hadn't been able to breathe well for months due to congestive heart failure. Six months ago, I took him through a labyrinth of stressful veterinary medical procedures to ease his breathing, but two days after, his symptoms returned.

We could have done it again. We could have submitted to another terrifying day of waiting rooms and needles, but how many times until we accept the inevitable?

Since the death of my husband in 2008, I have had an uneasy relationship with the medical system anyway. When they told us Dave had leukemia, his only symptoms were some lethargy and pain in his side. He checked into the hospital as prescribed for treatment. The chemotherapy made him much, much sicker. His immune system destroyed; he got pneumonia. Everything he had feared happened in that hospital, and despite a host of invasive medical treatments, he didn't get better.

The outcome was exactly the same as if he had refused treatment, except he died in the hospital instead of at home. Is it any wonder I rejected more medical treatment for Spot?

What should a competent person do when essentially powerless? I tried to arrange for Dave to die in the home he loved, but the doctors told me he couldn't be moved. He had been in that damn hospital for six straight weeks. I signed all sorts of paperwork, told the doctors what I thought he would want, even brought in a committee of resources, but my best efforts couldn't save him, couldn't spare him the trauma of treatment, couldn't even bring him home to die.

How many times until I accept the inevitable? How many times before I accept my own limitations?

I could spend every day of Dave's illness at his side, but I couldn't follow him wherever he went in death. To this day, this confuses me.

I could house, feed, and play with Spot, and even dig his grave. But I could not carry him to an easier death at the vet against his will. He hated going to the clinic and hid under the couch when I brought out the carrier.

Simply put, I could not give him up without his consent.

Did I fail them? I don't know. God knows I would have given anything to ease their way, but willingness doesn't make something possible. It wasn't my journey. That power was beyond my capabilities.

Perhaps part of love is the willingness to suffer on behalf of the beloved, even if you can't take the pain away. It will have to be enough. We can only give what we have.

May you both rest in peace. In the sum of things, you brought me more joy than pain. I'm still here, I remember you, and I promise to make the best of everything you taught me.

Unexpected Grace

When you keep chickens, occasionally, you open the coop and discover a chicken has died overnight.

It's sad.

You extract her little body from the pine shavings, and if it's not winter, you bury her in the little graveyard. In winter, when the ground is frozen, you'll have to take her remains to the pet memorial center. There you'll tell the attendant stories about her while you fill out the intake form.

It's hard, but you can't turn back time. God brings chickens into the world, and God takes them out. You might offer some assistance by dispatching a bird with an incurable disease or even processing meat chickens, but you didn't make the system, and you can't change it either.

You can't make the chickens live forever by confining them. They want to roam. They want to scratch up the ground, and eat the bugs, and flap their wings. If you let them, they'll make you laugh and follow you around the yard in an endless, joyful search for food.

They know about the hawks and the raccoons, and they mitigate the risk in their own ways. Yet, you won't find them hiding all the time.

I took the risk of quitting my job; I took the risk of loving new friends, animal and human, and daily I take the risk that something will go wrong. I take risks with the full knowledge that risk is the only path available.

The imaginary bargain that I will avoid risk and Life will spare me pain isn't real. It's just a distraction, one of many meant to make you forget that the very act of living is risky. In truth, something bad can happen at any time.

And sometimes it does.

But mostly, it doesn't.

Most of the time, you open the coop door, and all the chickens come out.

Most of the time, the sick bird gets better and lives to steal your sandwich again.

And even when she doesn't, you know, she had a good time while she was here and that it's OK.

She's just making room for something new.

Blog: "Raccoon Time" June 9, 2016

Summertime on the Homestead is a time of activity, especially in June. The sun rises early, and all the birds start shouting with glee.

"Let us out!" shout the chickens, pecking at the coop door outside.

"Hey! This is my food!" shout my doves at each other in the room next door.

"Get up!" calls old Glory the Cat, "It's time to feed me!"

The younger cats snooze until I pull myself out of bed. We were up late, and we are tired.

I start the coffee, feed Glory, and stumble outside to let the chickens out. I count them while they scatter. Eight, the same number I counted at Chicken Bedtime the night before. I sigh with relief.

Patience the Cat, and I look around. The garden fence is disturbed; the catch bucket at the faucet is overturned, and we find a dropping.

We know who is responsible.

The night before, we had heard rattling and scratching noises. I had gotten out of bed and opened a window to find a mama raccoon and five kits, still about a third her size. She led them around the yard, digging and thrusting her nose into the straw to find food while the kits tried to figure out how to get over the garden fence. One by one, they learned to climb the fencing and joined her.

Like anybody who keeps chickens, I get nervous when raccoons hang out in my yard. A raccoon will kill the whole flock and only eat one. Coops have to be reinforced against them, and I have a strong bias against their presence. In fact, Georgia Chicken got stolen by a raccoon last year. It's a "natural death for a chicken," as one friend consoled, but I'm still angry and don't like to see them in the yard. I keep a saucepan full of rocks near the window and shake it to scare them away whenever I see one.

I didn't shake the saucepan this time, though. Since they showed no interest in the chicken coop, I shut the window and went back to bed.

We were awakened later by squealing, squeaking, and security lights. The young cats and I all looked at the window and then at each other. I opened the window again.

The raccoons must have found enough to eat because they were playing! The mama raccoon was tussling with the babies. She would chase them and nuzzle them with her nose while they wriggled and squealed. She jumped up on a tree, and jumped down again, and ran around while they chased her. Sometimes she would play with one kit while the others gamboled around together like kittens.

I was stunned.

When I think of raccoons, I think of hardware cloth, cement blocks, and double-locked coop doors. I didn't know they could play. I didn't know their mothers took pleasure in raising them.

In a few weeks, those kits will be grown up. They'll be a danger to my chickens, and I'll do my best to lock up the food, empty the water bucket, and scare them away.

But just for right now, I'll watch this little miracle in disbelief and smile when I am woken up by joyful squealing.

Chapter 4: Every Little Chicken

Did you know you can use up all your hope?

During the six weeks between Dave's diagnosis and death, I got an interesting education in the nature of hope. We squeezed every last bit of it out of a difficult situation.

At first, we hoped the diagnosis was wrong.

Then, we hoped it was a mild case.

When it turned out to be serious, we hoped the chemotherapy would work. We hoped the various numbers and markers and dials would show that Dave was getting better.

I remember the night he started to show signs of pneumonia. A technician came in to take the usual numbers, blood pressure, blood oxygen, and temperature.

"His blood oxygen is pretty low," this person commented.

"Should I get a nurse?" I asked, relying on my usual hyper-competence to keep myself calm.

He said yes. I raced around the floor, trying to get someone to pay attention. Incomprehensibly, I had to go back more than once. I was too polite, and they didn't understand the urgency.

A nurse finally came in, and I retreated to the back of the room, watching numbly as they confirmed the seriousness of the situation and brought in more personnel and more equipment. I could feel the hope that he would come home evaporating as he was absorbed into the machinery of the hospital.

And yet, I redoubled my efforts. I went home, telling myself it was all a false alarm, and he would be fine the next day. I even went to work in the morning and tried to concentrate until a friend who worked in the hospital called.

"Dave has been moved to the ICU," he explained gently. "You should come down here."

Two Weeks

Dave was in the ICU for what were the strangest two weeks of my life.

Day after day, I would go to the hospital, only to sit in the waiting room. Friends visited. I put together monthly reports for my job, a thing that seemed odd to other people, but it was an island of normalcy in a sea of horror to me.

Dave couldn't breathe and had an oxygen mask at first. He would try to take off the mask to tell me things, and

I would make him put it back on, something I still half-regret. He couldn't breathe, and the mask made him feel better, but what would I give now to find out what he was trying to say?

Eventually, the doctors put him on a ventilator. A ventilator includes a tube that goes down the patient's throat and into his trachea so that the machine can push oxygen into his lungs. That was the end of any talking.

He had been at the end of his chemotherapy regimen and had no immune system.

We hoped and hoped for a miracle, but he didn't get better.

The Seed

I carry with me just one sparkling seed of real hope from that time.

One day, I came into Dave's ICU room to find a teddy bear and a flannel blanket with a note.

"What's this?" I asked the nurse.

"Oh," he said casually. "When someone donates white blood cells to a leukemia patient, they bring a bear and a blanket. It's an anonymous donation, so they don't know if the patient is a child."

I still have that blanket, and whenever I see it, I'm reminded of how stunned I was by this information.

Do you understand what that means? It means that in our world there are people who are so kind, so generous, that they will risk their convenience and even their own health to help someone they will never meet, someone who could live or die without a whisper of recognition. The nurse explained to me that donors of white blood cells take a drug that causes them to produce more of these cells, and then they donate them to people like Dave, people they don't even know.

I couldn't plant that seed for years…, but to this day, I pause with wonder when I think about it.

Blog: "Chickens; Life and Death" September 5, 2013

Wednesday, September 18th is going to be an odd day.

Many of you know that 9/18 is the anniversary of my late husband's death. He died five years ago, and it's an old story now, but I'll explain it for those who didn't know. He got leukemia out of nowhere when he was 45 years old and died within six weeks of the diagnosis.

Every year I try to figure out how to mark the anniversary of his death. I don't like to put too much emphasis on it because his death was only the end of his life and a difficult time for us both. I like to celebrate his birthday with more fanfare because that seems like a better way to remember what a

*positive influence he was on my life and how happy I am that
I got to spend twelve years with him.*

*My life is completely different than it was five years ago. I
moved to Colorado and learned to do things for myself. I built
a life around things I love—farms, small businesses, and
animals.*

*Dave didn't think much about any of these things. He would
never have been comfortable with a bunch of landscape-
destroying, messy chickens in the yard. These things are
entirely mine.*

*That leads me to the second part of why September 18th will
be an odd day. This year, I will spend it helping out a
Chicken Processing Class. "Processing" is a nice word for
killing the meat chickens and turning them into food. It's an
emotionally difficult day and easier to talk about in
euphemisms.*

*That seems especially strange after the pictures of my
backyard chickens, doesn't it? They will not be attending the
class with me. Their lives will be the same that Wednesday as
they are today, though they may get a few extra treats.*

*I want to go to the class because death is really just a part of
life. We all die eventually, one way or another, expected or
not. Since I eat chickens (chickens I'm not personally
acquainted with), I feel it's important to act as a witness to
this part of their lives. It's hard to be present at a death, but I
don't want to shield myself from their reality.*

One of the farmers, and the teacher of the class, is also a widow. I told her how I will be bringing donuts because I like to mark the anniversary of Dave's death by eating them. I'm not a big fan of them, but he loved donuts.

"I love donuts, too," she said. "And that would be awesome. I'm glad you're willing to share something like that with us."

It will be an odd day, but a meaningful one. For me, it will be a reminder of the precarious reality of our lives and the friends who make it all worth it.

Frozen Future

Dave is frozen in our memories at age 45, but somehow, I'm still here and still having birthdays. I still have birthday cakes and have to remember to write the date with the right year in January.

You might be surprised at how much faith it takes to believe that the future will turn into a today.

For years, people would say things to me like, "What do you see yourself doing in ten years?"

I would stare at them blankly.

"I don't really think like that," I would say. "I like to see what opportunities come along and then choose a direction."

But it wasn't true.

The truth was that I had become fatalistic. Why set goals when the future is so precarious? Why bother with hope for the future? I had used up that line of thought, and it hadn't borne anything but grief.

Do you have any idea what your animals are planning for 2013?

We don't make resolutions around here. I recently learned the power of goal setting, and apparently, this practice has spread to the rest of the household. All week, I've been finding scraps of paper with goals written on them.

Here's one I found at the bottom of the cats' water bowl.

<u>Things I'd like to accomplish in 2013, my first full year as a cat</u>

- *Stop letting Pickles pull out my whiskers and grow them long enough to brush the floor when I walk*
- *Become King of the Chickens by running up to them and scaring them at least once a week*
- *Figure out how to get toys and other small items out of the water bowl without getting my paws wet.*

I can only surmise that these were written by Patience the Kitten. He tends to be wordy. I found another one that probably belongs to Mr. Pickles at the top of the cat tree where he sleeps.

<u>Goals for 2013</u>

- *Finish pulling out Patience's whiskers*
- *Clean the Food Bearing Monkey's face once and for all*
- *Sleep under the bedcovers at least once.*

And there were more! A member of the household found this one under a bed.

<u>Plan for 2013</u>

- *Stop my Food Bearing Monkey from ever leaving the house again by refining guilt tactics.*
- *Increase volume of lonely, pathetic meowing in the night.*
- *Perfect technique of rubbing against other bipeds and shying away when petted.*
- *Run downstairs and stare at my Food Bearing Monkey with big eyes to communicate a deficit of petting time whenever FBM comes home.*

We suspect that was Harley.

I've been impressed at the household cats' grasp of grammar and spelling! We found one more, written in childish paw.

*** Convince Uncle Patience to let me ride on his back at least once in 2013 before I get too big.

That had to be Chessy the Kitten. No one else would want to ride on Thundercat Patience's back while he careens around the house for fear of getting hurt!

I found a couple more scraps in the coop, this time with letters impressed into the paper with toenails. Apparently, the arrival of two new chickens a couple weeks ago caused more excitement than I realized.

This was in the old coop, Chicken Shantytown.

1. Attempt to make friends with the newcomer, Big Delaware Chicken (Editor's note: I think they are referring to Marshmallow, a 2-year-old Delaware)
2. If #1 fails, eat Big Delaware Chicken
3. Resist abandoning Chicken Shantytown, despite the abundance of snacks in the new coop

I knew they were determined to stay in the old coop, but I didn't realize how determined!

And finally, I found this written on a bit of shell in the new coop, presumably by Marshmallow and Roxanne, the newcomers.

*** Figure out where the heck we are.

I guess it's hard to have nothing more at your disposal than a tiny chicken head to figure out what's going on in your life. At least they have a goal. It will keep them busy until 2014.

Who Cares?

Everyone has to come up with their own answer to the big questions.

Why am I still here?

Who cares?

To find the answer to that question, I decided to search the religion of my birth, Judaism, and try to discover if God cared one way or another. For years, I was so angry at God that I couldn't bring myself to acknowledge anything Jewish. I avoided holidays. I refused to light Shabbat candles. I made a habit of eating bacon.

I just didn't have any evidence that God cared.

To my way of thinking, I had celebrated all those holidays before Dave died and lit all those candles only for the sake of being part of the community. I thought Judaism's focus was on getting along with others and that God didn't notice the individual.

I thought God had made a system, dropped us into it, and that His concern was keeping the system going, nothing more.

I was wrong about that.

In time, I picked up Rabbi David Wolpe's book, *Healer of Shattered Hearts,* and found within it a revelation.

God could see me!

Just as I had painfully witnessed the deaths of the meat chickens, thus assuring that their short lives mattered to someone, God witnessed Dave's death and my struggles to survive. We weren't just a bit of hardware in some sort of cosmic machine running a spiritual quality assurance test.

Rabbi Wolpe made exactly the point I needed to hear. All I had known was that Judaism is a multifaceted religion that gives a lot of weight to action. Of the 613 commandments, many of them are directives about what to do in specific situations. For example, we are obligated to return lost objects and refrain from embarrassing someone in public.

Judaism also has a bond with the state of Israel, another concrete aspect of our spirituality.

I knew about all that, but what does Judaism say about God? I didn't know because my religious education in the Reform Jewish system hadn't had much to say about God. Don't be too hard on us. After the Holocaust, the questions were too big, and no answer made sense. It's too hard to think about, and I think some of us dropped the subject for a while.

Luckily, our ancestors thought about God a lot. Rabbi Wolpe's book brought that rich history to my attention.

With that began a journey of building a better relationship between myself and the Master of the Universe. I set out to learn what religious people knew, just as I had set out to learn what the farmers knew. This time, instead of getting more farm animals, I listened and read extensively and found myself a local Orthodox Jewish rabbi to learn from.

You see, if this was the case, if God witnessed, and cared, and was with me in all that misery, then maybe I could see a future after all. Maybe the whole thing hadn't been meaningless, and I wasn't as alone as I felt.

If everything was being run by a God who could see me, then maybe I wasn't living in a cold and thoughtless universe. If the universe wasn't cold and thoughtless, then maybe there was some reason to do more than go through the motions of living—maybe there was a reason to participate in my own life.

This revelation didn't tell me the answer to my recurring question, "Why am I still here?"

What it did tell me is that an answer exists.

All I have to do is seek it out.

As fall begins and the daylight wanes, my chickens start molting and stop laying eggs. I haven't eaten an egg in weeks, but nature is seasonal. Earlier in the year, the peaches ripened, and we ate, cooked, and canned as many as we could. Later it was frozen beans and pickled cucumbers, but what all this produce has in common is a season that begins and ends. So it is with eggs. The chickens lay a few in the winter, peak in the summer, and stop in the fall.

Two years ago, I brought these four birds home as two-week-old chicks. When I told people I was getting chickens, we always had some variation of this conversation.

"Are you getting them as pets or for eggs?"

"Oh, they are livestock," I would reply. They'll provide eggs, and then I'll eat them when they get older."

The other person, especially if she had known me a long time, would smile indulgently and suggest I was more likely to open a Chicken Retirement Home.

Sure enough, the laying hens became pets, and I learned from farmers this isn't uncommon. A three-year-old hen of a breed known for egg production yields tough meat and a certain amount of sadness at slaughter. You've cared for her a long time and gotten to know her, and maybe she even has a name. It's hard to let her go. If you want meat, it makes more sense to buy a batch of "meat bird" chicks. They've been bred to mature in six weeks and, if not slaughtered, die of heart attacks soon after. It's easier to maintain an emotional distance, and you get the added advantage of meat that's good for more than stew.

The transition from livestock to pets began when I gave my chicks names. It happened naturally as I watched them grow, and I learned to tell them apart by the feather patterns on their heads. They became Redhead, Specklehead, Blonde Chicken, and because her head was somewhere between red and blonde, Middle Chicken.

When they grew into their feathers and out of the brooder, I built them a coop, affectionately referred to as "Chicken Shantytown." Chicken Shantytown consists of a long cage made of hardware cloth with homemade doors at both ends. I've boxed in four feet with plywood and straw to protect them from the weather and provide some privacy for laying eggs.

Technically, this 30 square foot coop offers enough space for four hens, but every morning they squawk at the door, dragging their beaks along the wire, like prisoners with tin cups.

"Let us out of Chicken Jail!" I imagine they are saying. "We're innocent!"

They are. And so, I do.

All day long, my little bird friends roam around the backyard, doing what chickens were born to do. They run *around and flap their wings. They eat all the kitchen scraps in what used to be the compost pile. They hold meetings under the deck. They make me laugh and remind me how to greet every day as an opportunity for something good.*

And don't forget about the eggs.

During the summer, they gave me so many eggs I started tipping service providers with them.

"Here's the check for the invoice, and these fresh eggs are for you," I'd say, starting yet another conversation about the novelty of keeping chickens in the city.

"What made you decide to get chickens?"

"I can't explain it," I always say. "It seemed like the right thing."

In this middle season of my life, I want the simplicity and quiet to hear God speak. I want to live like the chickens, expressing the best of my nature. I'd had enough of the rat race and its mirage of success. I wouldn't trade my homestead and the chickens for any of its offerings.

Every day, they remind me to be grateful for that freedom.

Freedom

I found another kind of freedom. The freedom to live as if everything will be alright.

Dave's death brought home to me that we can't really be 100% sure that we'll be alive tomorrow. We like to believe we will, and maybe we have to believe that in order to be able to plan for tomorrow.

But believing that is not faith. It's just a helpful illusion.

Faith is something else.

After everything I've experienced, it seems to me, realistic faith means living a life that has meaning. Faith means having the courage and the spiritual authority to do what you think is right, even when it's not popular, expected, or understood by the people around you.

With faith, you can believe you are part of something bigger than yourself so that you can act with the responsibility of making the most of the gifts you've been given, even if that means making hard choices.

Let me give you an example. I used to date a lot and cycled through several relationships after Dave's death. I would follow the conventional wisdom and let my heart make decisions about how close I would let each boyfriend get.

The result? I was angry all the time, and anger takes up valuable energy. I had to learn that I am not suited to casual relationships. If I was going to accomplish anything, then I would have to protect myself. I began dressing like a religious woman and insisting on following religious rules of modesty when interacting with men.

I know for some people, that is a controversial thing to do, but that's my point. God has given me resources to do something important, and I needed to protect myself to preserve those resources. I did what I needed to do, and I've gotten into plenty of arguments about it with people who think my way of life is a criticism of them.

To me, that's faith. It means acting as if we are each a part of something larger than ourselves. That even though our lives are brief and uncertain, our actions matter. Maybe we have to take stands that other people don't like, but the approval of others is not the end goal.

The end goal is to become the best possible version of ourselves because we know it matters to something bigger than us. That if we set our minds to it, we will be able to do something that matters, despite the uncertainty of living another day.

This, I think, is what the farmers knew. It's not all about us. Life is full of risk and loss and unexpected instability, but it still matters what we do and who we are. We have a role to play in this temporary drama we're all part of, regardless of what we may suffer, and it's best to acknowledge that reality and get on with the work. We can stay in bed, refuse to eat, and decline to

participate, but we won't heal that way. It only wastes
time.

It's best to live as if everything is fine, try not to think
about the inevitable losses, and make the most of the
time we have. We need to make hay while the sun
shines.

Goal Setting

Did I do it? Did I find a way to set goals and make the
most of my time?

Did I learn to believe that tomorrow was a real thing
and that I had a future?

Yes and no.

To be honest, I still struggle with believing in the
future, but I can believe in the present. I had to start by
trying to make each day meaningful. I did this in
various small ways.

For years, I wrote a blog that promoted local businesses
and farms. I love talking to people, and having a way to
help people market their businesses was very satisfying
to me. I positioned myself as the translator between
farm life and city life so that people could understand
where their food came from and how hard it is to get
that food.

I do other small things. I make a point of encouraging people and giving them any positive feedback that comes to mind. I noticed how this can make a big difference in a person's day or even life.

To this day, I do things like lending out my old truck to friends with cars out of commission or hiring people for small tasks when they need money.

It helps to focus on other people. After all, nothing in my experience says that no one else has a future. It's just me who has a tenuous hold on it.

Knowing that God is encouraging me along, I can piece my life back together, as if the future is a real thing. I call myself the "Purveyor of Harebrained Schemes" because I'm full of ideas. It makes sense if you think about it. I don't think God would have granted me so many blessings if I wasn't here to do something big.

Inexplicably, I've been granted health and enough money, and friends and parents who have lived long enough to help their grown daughter through this journey. I think it's amazing that after all my ancestors suffered, I live in a peaceful time with a cornucopia of resources.

How could it be anything but my responsibility and obligation to do something important?

What will I do?

Why am I still here?

I'd like to share what I've learned with other people. Every one of us has the power to make new decisions and live as though what we accomplish matters.

I want to share what I've learned from my father about meaningful work and the concrete skills that shape our lives into what we want them to be.

I've learned to set goals in small bites. I can now get my head around the steps that bring a vision to life.

I don't know how it will turn out, but I'm well suited to solving life's puzzles.

After all, it's not a big jump from not believing in the future to being comfortable with not knowing where the path leads.

As long as God sees me, I can live.

Letter to Rabbi W

I am a stranger to you, as you are to me. You mention in your book, <u>Why Faith Matters</u>, that one doesn't necessarily know a person from his public writings, and I know this to be true. Sometimes it is even true that a person who does know you overestimates the insight into your condition from your writings. That was best demonstrated by a conversation I had with my mother once.

Mom: "I read the depressing essay of yours they posted this morning! Are you okay?"

Me: "Oh, yes. I wrote that last week. I have to go now. I'm due at the opening of a new cupcake shop."

I make this point that I am writing from stranger to stranger because sometimes only a stranger, with all the unknowns of his character, has the power to put something into perspective.

I'm a 44-year-old widow who has been struggling with grief and responsibility for a long time. Thankfully, the community of middle-aged widows isn't very big, but that makes for an interesting and somewhat solitary journey. I've had to find my own way to live with the impossibility of Dave's death and the equally impossible reality that I am still living.

"We have different jobs now," I told him when the doctors said it was time to let him go. "It's your job to find a way to die, and my job to find a way to live."

Dave did his job with inspiring grace. I'm still working on mine.

You would think the synagogue would be helpful in this matter, but I find its teeming activity of families lonely. I don't like to go. This year, the High Holy days approached, and I had to find a way to mark them, along with the fifth anniversary of Dave's death on September 18. The answer to *this puzzle came from a friend, another widow of my age, and a local farmer.*

This year, on Yom Kippur and again on the anniversary, I helped out at chicken processing classes on her small farm. I know this seems odd, but the connection of life and death always shimmers on the surface of a farm; and I can think of no better place to face the vibrancy of life and its corresponding mortality.

This was the first time I'd ever been present at slaughter, which I could only bear to watch from the kitchen. I was present at the death of my late husband, and I've written essays, and will no doubt write more essays, about the spiritual impact (impact is the right word) of witnessing the death of one of God's creatures. I felt that same sharp sense of loss for my friend's chickens.

I'm sure I'll feel it at all the future losses, too, losses of pets and parents and friends that are sure to come if I live long enough.

The inevitability and the recurring sharpness of grief is, of course, completely unbearable, but two of your sermons (which I listen to on podcast) have been especially helpful in helping me find a way to think of it. The first was entitled "Why you may not hide." I don't know if it occurred to you when you wrote it that the importance of really seeing the suffering of others, even if you can't or aren't going to do anything about it, might apply to chickens. It did occur to me. And in the other, a more recent sermon about the power of memory, you made the point that God remembers even when we can't.

I burst into tears when I heard that last statement.

What I heard is that God knows and sees and remembers every little chicken, even if I can't bear to do it myself. He remembers the now-deceased cats my late husband and I cherished, even if I no longer see their ghosts flitting about at the edges of my vision. And though I can't remember Dave's voice anymore, though I've made my happy, post-widowhood life something thoroughly of my own creation, and though that life is far removed from our shared past, God remembers when I can't.

Because God sees and remembers, I am free to live. I am free to make space for new loves, be they people or animals or a way of life.

You mentioned, in another sermon, that God wants us to be grateful. I can do that. I can't remember everything or personally witness the death of every chicken or spare anyone from the inevitability of death, but I think I can manage gratitude.

If that's my job, if that's my share of the responsibility, I can handle living.

Sincerely,

Bonnie Simon

Conclusion: Chicken Faith

Aren't women sometimes compared to hens? No doubt, the idea comes from our similarities. Hens are usually found enjoying each other's company, and they talk a lot. I like to think there is more, though, or at least more to strive for.

We humans struggle mightily with faith, whether it's faith in ourselves, God, the Universe, or whatever. Chickens, on the other hand, are born with it.

The phrase *"to be chicken"* means to be afraid and unable to hold one's place in the world, which actually does not describe chickens at all.

Poultry know their place. They watch for hawks, foxes, and raccoons. They flap around excitedly at sudden noises or movements. They announce to each other that danger might be in the area. And then they do the unexpected.

They calm down.

They go right back to their happy chatter and Very Important Chicken business.

They run around, squawking happily in the rain, heedless of their wet feathers. They stream out of the coop when I step out of the house with a box of hen scratch, excited again, even though I gave them hen scratch ten minutes ago.

My girls know how to squeeze every last bit of joy out of their feathery lives. Their commitment to happiness never wavers. You'll never catch a chicken overanalyzing a situation. She'll react with the fullness of her poultry nature and take her chances.

They make a good point. What good does second-guessing ourselves do for us?

Skepticism and worry can drain the joy from our brief lives. Better to shamelessly be as God made us.

Better to chatter endlessly with your friends, and only stop to focus on the blessing of treats.

Better to squawk in the rain with everything you've got and let your heart sing at the first sign of spring.

Better to live with the faith of a chicken.

Epilogue

Are you wondering where I am now?

Everything has turned out fine, but in a completely unexpected way.

I had expected to be married again by the time I was 50, but that didn't happen.

I had expected Mr. Pickles and Mr. Patience would live for nearly 20 years and I wouldn't have to suffer through the loss of a beloved cat again for a long time, but that didn't happen either. My beloved Mr. Pickles passed on in 2023. As of this writing, my sweet Mr. Patience is still with us. He has his own cat now, Mr. Scout.

I had expected that I would make a living writing, whether it was books, blogs, or something else. Strangely, that didn't happen either. It turns out that I don't enjoy writing for a living nearly half as much as I thought I would.

I have nothing else inspirational to tell you. It's hard to be a person, as I always say, but I get through it by focusing on other people and the remarkable gifts I've been given. Going through loss with the support and tools of the religious community has made it much more manageable and less confusing than before.

The loss never really goes away, and every subsequent loss dredges up some of the previous losses, but it also highlights the miracles.

It was completely unexpected that eight of my neighbors would become the most cohesive, supportive community I have ever lived in. We became friends during the pandemic, and they have been with me at every step since then.

It was completely unforeseen that I would find so much satisfaction in providing a place for people to live in the form of renting part of my house. Watching my various housemates rest from broken relationships, build up toward their goals, and even being a kind of substitute mom to young traveling professionals makes me happy.

It was completely unexpected that I would find myself working as an Auto Broker and discovering that it's the best job I've ever had!

You wouldn't think selling cars would give a person so many opportunities to help others. However, I don't work at a regular dealership. The business model puts me in a position to help lots of people with a purchase that is normally a stressful chore. We make it easy to understand and fun, and lots of my clients become friends. It's a great fit for a sociable person who likes to help other people get what they need.

My business takes me into the social world, and I get to know lots of people, something I enjoy and would do even if I didn't need to make money. It provides me with enough income to support all those chickens and to support other people by deliberately giving charity.

It's a great life. Simple, but not easy; not always happy, but full of joy and satisfaction. It's everything I could ask for.

It's a life lived with the faith of a chicken.